Ascending: Practical Advice for Women in Law and Business

SHERRI DAHL

DEDICATION

To Darlena, Kodee, Jagger, and Joel.

CONTENTS

1
INSPIRATION FROM LEGENDARY WOMEN

"I figure, if a girl wants to be a legend, she should just go ahead and be one." Calamity Jane.

In ten years, I changed from a 27-year old, barely educated, divorced, single mother of two, living on a military base in the middle of the Mojave Desert, to a lawyer working on the 42nd floor of a high rise, in an enormous international law firm, on the other side of the country. Ten years after that, I left big firm law practice, took a giant leap of faith, and began working for myself as Dahl Law LLC in the corner of my living room. How did all of that happen? It was and continues to be a journey fueled by inspiration from friends, colleagues, women in history, and the little voice in my head.

During free moments, I look for inspiration from other women who stepped out in faith or who overcame obstacles. These women did not sit around waiting for a prince to sweep them off of their feet (I enjoy the Cinderella story as much as the next girl, but a fairytale is not a reliable business model, unless you write the book, which is later turned into a movie). The women described in this book did not accept negative treatment and feel rejected and unworthy . . . at least not for long. They all overcame extreme obstacles. They did not wait for others to reward them with a title, fame, or money. They created the titles, earned the fame by their own actions, and made their own money.

If you ever have a day when you are feeling low, depressed, or like the world has been unfair to you, think about Calamity Jane. Born Martha Jane Cannary on May 1, 1852, both of her parents died when she was a teenager in the wild west.[1] In 1865, Calamity Jane's mother, father, and five siblings left Missouri by wagon train headed for Montana. Her mother died during the trip. A year later, Calamity Jane's father died. Without any of the niceties that we take for granted today (you know, like indoor plumbing) Calamity's Jane's survival in the 1800s is a testament to her grit. Some think that she exaggerated stories of bravery, but no one doubts that Calamity Jane drank whiskey and cussed . . . a lot. In her early years, she was a dancer in a dance hall and may have been a prostitute. In her later years, she cooked and cleaned for prostitutes in a brothel. During her adventurous life, she also reportedly scouted for the military, helped the sick, performed in traveling western shows and was very skillful using guns, out-shooting most men. A Captain in the military reportedly gave her the name Calamity Jane in the context that Jane was a person you would want to have around in a calamity. She is described as "dressing like a man" because she wore pants, and during the time she spent with the military, she wore a military uniform (once again, pants), but there are also pictures of Calamity Jane, young and old, in dresses. This is a woman who did and wore what worked best for her despite external expectations. She was illiterate but we know about Calamity Jane, today, because of an autobiography pamphlet she dictated that was distributed to promote her appearance in a western show. Today, Jane would be on social media, speaking her tweets into her phone. She survived, you might even say thrived, in an era that was much more of a man's world than what we experience today.

Compared with Calamity Jane, how do women today fare? Modern statistics related to the advancement of women in the legal field, which primarily focus on promotion of and pay to women in the largest firms, haven't changed much in the last twenty years. For non-white women, the statistics have been and remain dismal. For example, The Ninth Annual Survey by the National Association of Women Lawyers reported in 2015 that lawyers of color represent only 8% of equity partners (that 8% includes men and women of color).[2]

Statistics related to the success of black American women in the late 1800s were more depressing, but that did not stop one ambitious women. Sarah Breedlove, born December 23, 1867 in Louisiana, later became known as Madam C.J. Walker, and is credited as the first female self-made millionaire in America.[3] Walker was the first child in her family born into freedom. Her mother and father had been slaves prior to the Emancipation Proclamation, which was issued January 1, 1863. Both died when Walker was 7. She lived with her older sister until she was married at 14. Her husband died when she was 20 and her daughter was 2. Walker moved to Missouri, where her brothers were barbers; she worked as a washer woman (laundry maybe?); she earned a dollar a day on a good day. Later, Walker sold hair care products for others until approximately 1905, when she moved to Colorado and married Charles Joseph Walker, a newspaper and advertising salesman. She coined the name Madam C.J. Walker and became an independent hairdresser and retailer of cosmetic creams. As her business grew, she trained women to sell products and to become "beauty culturists". Her daughter, A'Lelia Walker, headed up the mail order portion of the business in Colorado, and Walker opened Lelia College in Pittsburgh, Pennsylvania. In 1910, the headquarters of the operation opened in Indianapolis, Indiana. Walker organized her sales agents into clubs locally, statewide, and in other provinces. Walker's business expanded to include Cuba, Jamaica, Haiti, Panama, and Costa Rica.

Compared to what women in the past have had to overcome, our success should be relatively

4

easy, right? Unlike our grandmothers, we have access to birth control options and technology enabling us to work next to a crib, or in my case because my children are grown, a dog bed, or the bed of an aging parent.

In an article published November 14, 2015,[4] Ruth Bader Ginsburg, in her 80s, talked about cases on which she worked at the A.C.L.U., early in her career, where young African-American women were being sterilized without their permission during other procedures. Gloria Steinem, also in her 80s, featured in this same article, discusses attending college at Smith, an all girl's college, where it was widely known that women were being educated to produce educated children, not to accomplish their own ambitions. Ginsburg talks about how all nine of the Harvard law women in her class of 500, gathered to meet the dean who asked "How do you justify taking a spot from a qualified man?" Ginsburg graduated number one in her class, but describes her job search as very difficult because she had three strikes against her: she was a woman, who was Jewish, and she had a 4-year old daughter. Sign-up sheets for firms would say "Men Only". When Steinem sought a job at Time magazine, she was told that women researched and men wrote. And yet, these women achieved tremendous success. Steinem started Ms. Magazine, published several books, and for many represents the modern women's movement. Ginsburg became the second woman on the U.S. Supreme Court and through that position greatly impacts the law governing men and women.

Do our daughters realize that our grandmothers were many of the "first women" to accomplish certain tasks? Do they know what our mothers had to overcome? Naomi Sims was born in Oxford, Mississippi on March 30, 1949.[5] After Sims' parents divorced, when she was 13, she moved with her mother and two sisters to Pittsburgh, Pennsylvania, where her mother was forced to put her into foster care. In college, she won a scholarship to the Fashion Institute of Technology in New York City, while also taking classes in psychology at night at New York University. Sims' attempted modeling through agencies but was rejected; she was told that her skin was too dark. However, while still a teenager, she became a worldwide recognized model. Her breakthrough came when she decided to go around modeling agencies and work directly with fashion photographers. Gosta Peterson, a photographer for the New York Times, photographed Sims for the cover of the paper's 1967 August fashion supplement. After that success, Sims still had difficulty getting work. So, once again, she ignored the traditional process and forged her own way by sending copies of the Times supplement directly to advertising agencies, attaching Wilhelmina Cooper's contact information. Wilhelmina Cooper was a Dutch model who founded her own modeling agency. Sims told Cooper that if she obtained work, Cooper would receive a commission. Within a year, Sims was earning $1000 a week; she became the first black model on the cover of Ladies' Home Journal magazine in November 1968 (the year that I was born). Sims was also the first African-American model to appear on the cover of Life magazine in 1969. She went on to be a successful business woman and author.

Fashion magazines first began recognizing black women on covers, during my lifetime, so I suppose I should not be surprised that it has only been in the last twenty years that women have been promoted to partner in many law firms. In the last handful of years, some firms have begun appointing their first women managing partners. Progress is slow. Changing society takes time.

Throughout centuries, women have achieved success by contradicting tradition, creating their own business plans bucking conventional wisdom, and by moving forward in faith. Each successful woman has her own reasons for seeking higher goals and works hard to further her agenda. The importance of encouraging the next generation to follow their non-traditional dreams is crucial.

Hearing the stories of women who have achieved their goals inspires me to reach a little further to achieve what might seem impossible. Every day, on Facebook[6], I am reminded of the achievements of today's women by their posts, and the successes of historic women by the posts of The National Women's History Museum (NWHM)[7]. Located in Alexandria, Virginia, the NWHM "affirms the value of knowing Women's History, illuminates the role of women in transforming society and encourages all people, women and men, to participate in democratic dialogue about our future." More information about the NWHM and many other historic women can be found on the NWHM Facebook page and at www.nwhm.org.

As I mentioned earlier, in June 2015, I began a hike on a path in the legal industry that is mostly statistic free. I formed my own firm, Dahl Law LLC, and began working from home. I have not found any statistics reporting the success of women who work for themselves at home or who head up small firms. I can report to you only statistics related to my firm, so far. At Dahl Law, a woman is the 100% founder, owner, and management committee. After being a corporate bankruptcy attorney for most of my legal career, I decided to leave the large firm business model which had been my home for so many years. It felt like jumping off of the tallest building. As someone who researches buying a refrigerator for a year, leaving the security of a regular paycheck was daunting. It made no logical sense, but the little voice in my head, a voice I rely on often, said that everything would work out OK. In June, I had one client I thought might stay with me when I formed Dahl Law — a client in the final stages of a matter. In less than six months, I had helped 20 clients.

Are you happy in your current work environment? I am incredibly happy now. Working at home is not for everyone. Working at a huge firm is not for everyone. Regardless of where you work, my best advice is this: At work, or even if you are looking for a job, you should approach any project as if it is a project you are performing to benefit your own business (while at the same time, of course, helping your client or customer, if you have one). Do not simply do what others tell you to do. Always think to yourself: How can I best accomplish my personal business goals? This will guide you in determining which projects to accept or reject. At a firm, you may not be able to reject work, but you can choose whether you actively seek a particular type of work. You are always in charge of yourself, even when you work for someone else. It is not easy and sometimes there is an element of risk in bravely taking action to benefit yourself. Think about Calamity Jane, Madam C.J. Walker, Ruth Bader Ginsburg, Gloria Steinem, Naomi Sims, and Sherri Dahl — all followed Calamity Jane's wise words: "if a girl wants to be a legend, she should just go ahead and be one."

2
CREATE YOUR OWN PATH

Women are half the population, yet professional women are rarely half of any category in their respective industries. For example, statistics for women lawyers reflect the lack of female representation at the highest levels of law firms and business. According to a 2011 survey on the nation's 200 largest law firms prepared by The National Association of Women Lawyers, women comprised:

5% of managing partners -- these women lead an office or the entire firm;

15% of equity partners -- these are powerful owners of the firm with clients of their own;

25% of non-equity partners -- in a large firm,

non-equity "partner" promotions occur later and later. When I graduated law school in 2000, partner promotions were expected after 8 years; now these promotions occur after 10 or 12 years, or not at all;

55% of staff attorneys -- these are attorneys who work reduced hours for reduced pay or are not on the partner track;

34% of counsel -- typically, these are attorneys who have not been promoted to partner, but who are more experienced than associates;

47% of 1st and 2nd year associates; and

45.9% of all law school graduates.[8]

Many reports, like this one, conclude that women are disadvantaged, lack sufficient opportunity for advancement to the highest levels of the largest firms, and focus on encouraging firms to implement concrete steps that will assist greater numbers of women lawyers to advance their careers. I applaud every firm that focuses on assisting women's advancement.

That said, we do women a dis-service if we

focus only on what institutions and other people can do to help women ascend up the career ladder. It is nearly impossible to achieve promotion in a large law firm without some form of sponsorship from others. However, rather than encouraging women to look for a handout, instead I want to tell young women how to be more independent. I want to tell them "Look how far we have come!" and "You are the master of your own destiny – GO FOR IT!" Make a plan for success and execute it!

A quick Internet search indicates that at least 22 countries have had women lead them as President or Prime Minister.[9] Do you think those 22 women wasted their time thinking about how to get someone else to promote them? I am going to guess "no". Let us quit focusing all of our attention on words like "bias" and "discrimination" that make women sound and feel like victims. When we describe women in firms as victims, facing daunting obstacles and dismal statistics, we weaken them and we fail to inspire them to see greatness.

Of course, some women are victim to abuse – I am not talking about those women. In contrast, many women have not been victimized by treatment rising to the legal level of abuse, but still wait for someone to hand them promotion and success on a silver platter. I refuse to think of myself as a victim.

Again, some women are victimized. For example, in the past, women were excluded from the practice of law, and when they were permitted to become licensed attorneys, firms were slow to hire them.

These days, issues regarding women's advancement are extremely complex – much too complex for complete coverage in this book. Today, the success of women in law can no longer be judged simply by the statistics of how many of us are in a particular position. The vast majority of women (and men) do not judge their success on whether they are the managing partner of their firm, the CEO of their business, or President of the United States, because they do not want that title. With that in mind, is it fair to take the statistic that 5% of managing partners are women and conclude that firms do not facilitate women becoming managing partners? If you want to become the managing partner of a firm, the sure fire way for that to happen is to start your own firm.

Unlike Abigail Adams in 1776, wife of future President John Adams, we do not live in an era where women are considered property by their fathers and husbands, unable to sign contracts, own property, keep earnings or have custody of children if divorced. No teacher ever told me that only boys need to learn long division, as was told to early women's rights advocate, Susan B. Anthony.[10] I applaud Anthony's solution to the long division problem; she taught herself and learned through homeschooling. There was an obstacle and she went around it.

Younger women may forget the transition in women's roles in the last few decades. One of my earliest memories, in 1973 when I was five years old, is of my father being angry with my mother for working at our church part-time. His mother lived 98 years and never worked outside the home. Even at five years old, I was aware of the women's liberation movement and the equal rights amendment that failed to pass.

The late Chief Judge Anne Workman, of the DeKalb Georgia Superior Court, gave a speech in 2008 reflecting on the advancement of women attorneys during her life.[11] That speech describes well the status of women in the law when I was five. Judge Workman graduated from Emory Law School in 1972; ten percent of her class was female. When Judge Workman joined the DeKalb Bar Association in 1973, she was the third woman to be a member of the organization and women were less than four percent of attorneys nationwide. In 1973, my father never would have guessed that his five-year-old daughter would become an attorney in a law firm much less own her own firm (he is very proud now).

Some women in large law firms are disappointed when they do not achieve more sooner. Most of the time, I just felt lucky to be allowed to work at the big firm. Getting in the door of a big firm was not easy. College, for me, did not occur directly after high school. Instead, I was in a hurry to work full-time and pay my own way (what was I thinking?). Young people want it all . . . and they want it now.

So, I left my home state of Ohio and moved to California with $200 in my pocket. Gas cost $1.59 a gallon at that time; it was 1986 and I was 18 years old. I drove my used Buick Skylark (the car my dad gave me) across country staying in only one hotel, because that is all I could afford. Staying with relatives, I found a job the first week, making $5.00 per hour performing data entry. I was married at 19 to a man I had known for six months. When I was 23, after being steadily promoted at the same company for five years, I hit a glass ceiling at my job. Gender did not create that glass ceiling. I was not college educated; new owners of the company told me that I would not be promoted further without a college degree. I started taking one college class at a time in the evenings. While I was in the college slow lane, between 1990 and 1994, across the U.S., women grew from 42.5% to 43.3% of law school classes.[12]

In the mid-nineties, it hit me: I control my destiny. I can change the path I am on. I can become one of those women going to law school. Believe it or not, it was the O.J. Simpson trial that changed my life for the better and inspired me to finish an undergraduate degree and go to law school.[13] It wasn't the lawyering or the courtroom drama that inspired me.

At that time, in 1995, I was living on a military base as the spouse of a Marine Corps infantryman. I worked two part-time jobs, evenings and weekends, as a board operator at a radio station on the weekends between midnight and 6:00 a.m. and, in the evenings, performing typing and other computer work for Bill Lavender, a man who conducted business out of his house. My children were four and one at the beginning of 1995. During the day, I typically mopped all the tile floors of our military housing, did dishes and laundry, planned meals, and read books – legal and spy thrillers borrowed from Bill. My husband and I were having marital troubles that related to his mental health, which probably at least partially related to his 12-year tenure with the Marine Corps and deployments to places like Somalia.

One day, during coverage of the O.J. trial, a pundit talked about how abused people train other people to treat them in a particular way. The example was given that when an abuser treats a victim badly, there are many people who will immediately leave. In contrast, others will stay and allow the abuse to happen. By letting the abuse happen, a victim is training people to treat them badly. To be clear, I was not being physically abused by my husband. Also, it is not the victim's fault when an abuser abuses. Instead, what I took away from this discussion was the concept that **I control EVERYTHING in my life because I control my reactions to all things**. Hand in hand with the concept that I control my reactions I also came to the conclusion that I needed to **make some plans**. Before that day, I didn't really make plans unless forced. Primarily, I drifted along reacting to things as they occurred. At 26 years old, there was no plan for my future other than just living day to day. These revelations about controlling my reactions and making plans hit me like a ton of bricks as I walked upstairs carrying a basket of laundry, in 1995, and continue to influence every day of my life.

Beginning that day, I hatched plans for my future. But I needed help, because in 1995, I was separated from my husband, the primary care

17

provider for two small children, and living in the middle of the Mojave Desert. How does a person travel from the middle of the desert to an office in the tallest building of a large city, and then to owning their own law firm? Not by waiting for someone else to advance them. Long story short, my mother moved in with me, taking care of my kids as I worked multiple jobs while attending college. I earned a bachelor's degree by age 29 and three years later, a law degree. There was no cushy high paying Summer Associate Attorney position for me; my jobs during law school were hourly internships with the government and a small litigation boutique. Again, I never felt like being a woman reduced my opportunities. There wasn't time to feel sorry for myself. I knew then, as I know now, that many women paved the way for me, like Annette "Nettie" Cronise Lutes, the first woman lawyer admitted to practice law in Ohio in 1873.[14]

Regardless of published statistics, any time I looked up a career ladder, I saw women in leadership positions in law firms, large and small. OK, there were usually not many women at the highest levels of the largest firms, but there were plenty of non-equity women partners, and at that time, I did not appreciate the difference between equity and non-equity.

Women today have more choices than ever and sometimes exercise their right to choose by electing not to travel the path of the most stressful job working the longest hours. Individual women define success differently. Women throughout history fought for our right to choose our destinies, whatever they may be. And there is more for us to do.

Despite the fact that my life philosophy focuses on women creating their own destiny, I admit that we cannot control everything. Sometimes we need help or luck. Judge Workman acknowledged that sometimes terrific career opportunities just come your way by sheer, blind luck. Oprah Winfrey has said that luck is preparation meeting opportunity.[15] I agree with Oprah and I believe that some are made lucky because of the generosity of others.

There have been several men and women who have gone out of their way to help me advance. In the legal profession, particularly in a large firm, people at the top must reach out to those on the lower rungs to help them up – this is sponsorship. I might never have had the opportunity to work at a large firm if not for Judge William T. Bodoh's sponsorship. The Judge dramatically altered my future by hiring me as his law clerk. He and I met when I was in law school and he knew I was a single mother attending law school the hard way (divorced, poor, and with children). For his federal clerkship, he could have hired a person from an ivy league institution or someone with better grades. Instead, he took a chance on me. I am forever in his debt. Not only did he help me individually, but he inspires me daily to help others advance themselves. A person can have a tremendous ripple effect on the future through one generous act.

Every day, I feel lucky and a responsibility to create my own destiny by making wise choices, building relationships, and helping others. Through the efforts of women hundreds of years ago, who fought for women's rights, we are in the door and have a place at the conference room table. Now, we create our own luck. And those who are already at the top have a duty to be agents of luck for others.

3
ACHIEVE SUCCESS AND PAY IT FORWARD

In the past 140+ years, women have moved from not being admitted to the practice of law in the 1870s to having three women on the U.S. Supreme Court at the same time. We are in law firms, government, courtrooms, the military and board rooms. Law firms that are not promoting women to the highest levels should take notice; your women are going in-house, rising to the highest levels of companies, and are making decisions about the hiring and firing of law firms. And they remember who helped them and who did not.

Retired Justice Sandra Day O'Connor has said that she remembers 40 law firms refusing to interview her after law school because she was a woman.[16] I met Justice O'Connor once. She exudes an aura of strength and is the only person in whose presence I was completely speechless. I have met three U.S. Supreme Court justices and the other two did not have the same impact. The O'Connor meeting occurred because a law school classmate clerked for Justice O'Connor and arranged for me and two colleagues to meet the Justice in her Washington, D.C. chambers. Face to face with the Justice, shaking her hand, I was awed by her place in history as the first woman to achieve the highest ranking legal position in the U.S. If I spoke, I do not recall it. My mind was blank. There were no words. People who know me will find that hard to believe. I only remember one part of the meeting. One of my colleagues said to the Justice, "That is a lovely blouse." She was wearing a shiny gold blouse with rows of black purses printed all over. O'Connor said something like "When I wear this, I feel like a bag lady." The Justice cracked a joke! I still couldn't speak.

The awe that stole my words came from standing in the presence of a woman who helped pave the way for all women lawyers to ascend to the heights of legal practice. Yet, when you consider her resume, she is not so different from the rest of us. What is clear is that she did not sit back and wait for anyone to hand her a title or promote her – she blazed her own trail.[17]   Born in El Paso, Texas, March 26, 1930, she married John Jay O'Connor III in 1952.   She received a B.A. and L.L.B. from Stanford University and raised three sons.   Her official Supreme Court biography provides that she served as Deputy County Attorney of San Mateo County, California from 1952-1953 and as a civilian attorney in the U.S. Army in Frankfurt, Germany from 1954-1957.   From 1958-1960, she practiced law in Maryvale, Arizona, and served as Assistant Attorney General of Arizona from 1965-1969.   She was appointed to the Arizona State Senate in 1969 and was re-elected to two two-year terms.   In 1975, she was elected Judge of Maricopa County Superior Court and served until 1979, when she was appointed to the Arizona Court of Appeals. President Reagan nominated her as an Associate Justice of the Supreme Court and she took her seat September 25, 1981.

What the official bio does not tell you is that O'Connor's first attorney job was a non-paying job she accepted after 40 firms rejected her, even though she graduated third in her Stanford law class (William Rehnquist was number one in her class).[18] She turned down a paying job as a legal secretary to accept the unpaid position as an attorney. Undeterred when firms would not meet with her, she eventually opened her own firm.   After entering

23

politics, she was the first female majority leader in the Arizona State Senate.

Looking back at the last 140+ years reminds us of how far we have come. In 1869 in Iowa, Arabella Mansfield, was the first woman who gained admission to the practice of law in the United States.[19] In that same year, Lemma Barkaloo becomes the first woman law student in the nation at the Law Department of Washington University in St. Louis.[20] When the Illinois Supreme Court denied Myra Bradwell admission to the bar, the Court thought it relevant in 1869 that, as a married woman, Bradwell would not be bound by contracts she made.[21] In 1875, when Lavinia Goodell was denied admission to the Wisconsin Bar, a Justice remarked: "It would be revolting to all female sense of innocence . . . that woman should be permitted to mix professionally in all the nastiness of the world which finds its way into courts of justice."[22]

The arguments for keeping women out of the legal profession in the late 1800s remind me of the arguments made in the not-so-distant past about keeping women out of the military combat roles. Women have been fighting throughout the ages along with men to live full and satisfying lives based in freedom. None have fought more than the women in our armed forces. During World War II, civilian women served as test pilots, flying aircraft before they would be flown in combat by male aviators.[23] As of April 2012, more than 800 female soldiers had been wounded in the wars in Iraq and Afghanistan.[24] In 2015, women made up approximately 15% of the U.S. active duty military.[25] Military women have served as medics and intelligence officers. They are in convoys and accompany infantry troops searching civilians. Yet, female officers with unacknowledged combat experience have, in the past, been denied career advancement. In January 2013, then Secretary of Defense Leon Panetta ordered the military services to study the issue of women serving in combat positions and develop an implementation plan, setting January 2016 as the deadline for lifting the ban on women in combat. On December 3, 2015, Secretary of Defense Ashton Carter announced that all combat roles in the U.S. military would be open to women.[26] Just like our legal system, our military hierarchy will be richer with the diversity of background and experience added by women and other minorities.

New York Times columnist Nicholas D. Kristof, in a piece titled "She's (Rarely) the Boss" (Jan. 26, 2013)[27], argues that women should be elevated to the highest levels of business because considerable evidence suggests that more diverse groups reach better decisions. Women are gaining ground in the largest companies. The article provides that 17% of American Fortune 500 board seats are held by women and 3% of board chairs are women. Kristof takes on some myths and argues that women at the top do not necessarily provide nurturing leadership (he says that women can be jerks too) and that women at the top will not always help other women. I agree.

In my lifetime, we have come a long way. In 1968, the year I was born, a property casebook published that year provided that "after all, land, like woman, was meant to be possessed[.]"[28] The number of women in leadership positions is rising . . . slowly. Yes, we have come a long way, but there are miles left to go. To get there, we must help each other. Women in positions of power should go out of their way to reach out and help other women up the ladder. If you are a powerful woman working in a company, call on women in law firms (and other businesses, like accounting), even if they are not exactly the specialized type of lawyer that you need. Generally, the person who gets the call gets the origination credit, even if she does not do the work -- she is credited with "having the relationship", which is valued highly within any firm. The woman you call will connect you with the best lawyer within the firm who can help you. Help other women get on boards. Nominate each other for awards. Let's not sit and wait for others to promote us. Ask for opportunities and higher salary. If your current employer is not willing to advance you, go somewhere else where they will -- or start your own firm. Like Justice Sandra Day O'Connor, we cannot let 40 rejections get us down. We have to overcome any obstacles in our path, achieve success, and then pay it forward.

4
CHANGING TIMES – THE NEW LEGAL MODEL

Dramatic changes in the business of law are transforming the way the legal industry operates. Firms and businesses slow to react to these changes will experience negative consequences. The old business model for large corporate clients involved retaining primarily large law firms and went something like this: A business needing legal help pays a premium to hire "the best" (usually the largest) law firm. That way, regardless of a legal outcome, the board for the company could say that they eliminated some amount of risk by relying on the best counsel available, because biggest means best (right?). The top 10% of law students (the best and brightest) had the opportunity to work in the largest, highest paying law firms and often did so.

The largest firms relied mainly on institutional clients that had been with the firm for many years and rarely had to worry about competition. Under the old model, legal departments for institutional clients were generally small and headed by older white men, who hired law firms based on relationships with people they could trust, who usually looked like them, went to school with them, lived near them, and played golf with them. Lawyers in the large firms worked around the clock on teams, loyal to the firm, knowing that someday, they would become partner and begin sharing in significant wealth. Business development was largely achieved when older partners retired and handed clients down.

In the last decade, a new model has emerged. Now, companies answering to shareholders, who have instant access to information, need to focus on costs (because this information is also easily accessible) and the best lawyers are not always at the largest firms. Today, large law firms do not hire as many first year attorneys as they did ten or fifteen years ago. Now, the top 5% of law students might have the opportunity to work in the largest firms. The large firms still cling to institutional clients, who now spread their work around to more than one firm. Clients are still willing to pay a premium for the best legal representation, but "the best" may not be the largest firm; it may be a boutique firm. With social media, electronic filing, and easier travel, the best firm may be the firm in another state, focusing on a particular type of case and marketing their capabilities through social media. Legal departments in companies are growing, because certain legal work can be handled more cost effectively in-house. Women are going in-house in droves because they (a) can rely on more regular workday hours; (b) are paid fairly, usually with better benefits; and (c) feel more upwardly mobile. Now, the person making decisions about which law firm should be hired is not necessarily always the highest ranking lawyer in a company's legal department; in-house lawyers at all levels retain firms and sometimes companies use hundreds of law firms in any given month. More and more women and people of color in-house are selecting where companies invest their legal dollars and they are picking people they trust, who are highly qualified . . . and who look like them. In a 2016 report, 56 Fortune 500 corporations have minorities as General Counsel, the highest legal position in a company, "an all-time high and a net gain of five from MCCA's previous survey."[29]

How are the large law firms reacting? Many cling to the old model, even though intellectually they must see that the old ways are not serving them as well as they used to. Perhaps they hope that previous years of reduced billable hours are a fluke or a symptom of a bad economy that will rebound, ushering in the return of the good old days. They do not realize that some of the changes that occurred in the last decade are sociological, related to a generation of lawyers, men and women, who at law firms and in-house (i) have greater access to information, (ii) have more power earlier in their careers, (iii) want to spend more time with their families, but have access to work while at home and on vacation, and (iv) are willing to change jobs as often as it takes to gain the type of work environment, pay and benefits they consider fair.

Now, although the best and brightest young lawyers may begin at large firms, they are not always staying there. Although new lawyers can feel good about advertised high salaries, their first year at a large firm, they learn quickly that salaries do not rise quickly after that, subsidized benefits are unheard of, attorneys without the highest billable hours are fired, and they may never make partner. And the best opportunities for gaining work experience are not always available at the largest firms. Simply stated, large law firms are getting less work from clients, resulting in large firms instituting cost-cutting measures allowing the wealthiest partners to continue receiving the expected large distributions. One such cost cutting measure is hiring fewer attorneys right out of law school. This is one of the biggest mistakes large firms make, because hiring fewer young lawyers inflates the hourly rates charged by the entire firm. When there are fewer low cost attorneys to push work down to, the remaining youngers attorneys are asked to perform lower level work (at higher cost to the client) and they do not enjoy working the longer less fulfilling hours. Hiring fewer new attorneys also makes large firms less diverse; when the total number of new hires is reduced, there is less opportunity for diversity.

In part, companies engaging lawyers will continue to do what they have always done. They will look for the law firms and lawyers who handle their individual needs the best. However, rather than assuming that those at the largest firms are the best, increased access to information through the Internet and social media will allow more direct information about successes from smaller firms to be accessed. Companies are learning that, now, the best and the brightest are not always at the largest firms and that bulky overhead of large firms drives up fees on all matters. More and more, attorneys at large firms are leaving the ivory towers because large firms no longer provide assurance of long term stability. In the wake of large law firm bankruptcies, attorneys must consider whether a firm will be viable in the long run and whether the firm culture will suit them as they enter their fifties and sixties. Likewise, clients are not staying with large firms the way they used to. In my experience, clients prefer the most responsive lawyers who they trust best.

Wise clients think in terms of who they want with them in the trenches on their worst days. Technology levels the playing field; no longer do large firms have the best access to information through their sheer numbers. Now, technology allows all lawyers, at large and small firms, whether working from home or in an office, quick access to the law and analysis of it. Companies and law firms, large and small, must think more like entrepreneurs – specifically, how to attract and engage the best talent. To achieve success in the modern world of the legal industry, every single lawyer, working in the smallest law firm or company or the largest, is an entrepreneur who must obtain access to the best and most recent information and use it. Firm lawyers must not only do good work, they must create a brand and market themselves. In-house lawyers working in companies have more opportunity than ever before to obtain the highest quality legal services while paying a fair price. Law firms and companies will thrive if they embrace the new legal model: a model where legal dollars spent provide lower cost results and are spread around to the most capable, wherever they are and whatever they look like.

5

IS SHIRTLESS UNDER A JACKET OK?

Taking a short break from servicing clients, I flip through the December 2014 edition of the American Bankruptcy Institute Journal magazine, featuring the scales of justice on the cover, and then I see it! On the inside front cover of the magazine is an ad showing a young, beautiful blonde woman with glossy lipstick, without a shirt. Yes, you read that correctly, I said without a shirt. She wore only a white suit jacket, pants, and an orange neck tie. The jacket exposed the woman's chest similarly to the way an evening gown would if cut down to the navel – something you might see Jennifer Lopez wear at the Grammy Awards. The caption on the ad said, "Worth Noticing." I flipped through every other page in the magazine, past all of the scholarly articles. The only skin in any other ad was a set of hands. In contrast, this ad, on the inside front cover, had 75% of a face, significant chest skin, and a partial breast.

Why do I hate this ad? If the ad were in Vogue or People magazines, it would not bother me. Why does it bother me in a legal journal? When I look at the ad, why do I feel sick to my stomach? I do not wake up each morning feeling powerless and oppressed as a woman lawyer. Quite the opposite – for most of my career I worked in large law firms, becoming a partner. Now, I own my law firm. Important people call and email me to ask my opinion about important matters. I have the freedom to come and go as I please and earn six figures. So, why does the ad distract and offend me?

After pondering for a couple of days, I conclude that I am offended primarily because the ad appears in a scholarly journal that I read at work. Secondarily, it reminds me of the subtle remaining sexism at the highest levels of business and law. In a magazine focused on reaching lawyers, I do not like seeing women pictured as sex objects. Put half-naked women in fashion magazines, where the body is the focus of most ads and articles. In legal magazines, I prefer women fully clothed – preferably in a judge's robe or the suit of a CEO.

I do not expect everyone to agree with me. Some of you will think I am over-reacting. I am going to go out on a limb and guess that the women who think the ad is harmless are probably younger than I am (younger than 48 years old). My thoughts on this subject are based on my experiences and my age. Raised by a single mother who told me that I could do anything, I started working when I was 14 and finished college later in life, after having two children. Law school began and ended after my divorce, thanks to my mom watching my young children. When I worked at manufacturing companies, before law school, I did not feel limited as a woman – although in my twenties I did have a very good job for several years working for a president and vice president who both kept calendars with pictures of naked women on their desks. The calendars were given to them by the female accounting manager. In law school and early in my legal career, in my thirties, I did not feel limited as a woman, I felt lucky to be a lawyer. However, in my forties, as I climbed the ranks and looked ahead to the highest levels of law firms and corporations, for the first time, I began to see and feel subtle limitations.

2020 Women on Boards (WoB) is an organization that conducts research studies about the gender composition of boards of directors of U.S.

companies.[30] Each year, 2020 WoB creates a Gender Diversity Index, based on the Fortune 1000 categorizing each company as: (a) winning, with 20%+ women on its board; (b) very close, with 11-19% women; (c) token, with 1 woman; or (d) zero, with 0 women on the board. In 2016, companies reported: (i) 50% were winning companies with 20%+ women on the board; (ii) 18% were very close; (iii) 25% achieved token status; and (iv) 8% maintained zero women on the board.[31]

Statistics related to women at the highest levels of the largest law firms are not much better. Although women are roughly half of all law school students, our numbers drop immediately after graduation, because we are only one-third of U.S. lawyers.[32] Another drop occurs at the partner level; woman make up only 18% of equity partners, up from 15% in 2011. The percentage of women leading large law firms drops to low single digits.

Selena Rezvani, in an article published in The Washington Post about women in law provides that:

> As an advisor to corporate women's networks, I am hard pressed to name an industry that simultaneously has more progressive policies and yet

more of an old-school culture than
the large law firm environment does.
You can draft as many pro-employee
policies as you like, but unless
women are co-creators in the firm's
strategy, they will not shape the
culture.[33]

Why aren't more women at the highest levels
of law firms? There are many reasons, including the
difficulty of learning exactly what needs to be done
to achieve elevation at a firm and the necessity of
having a sponsor willing to fight for your promotion.

In the years that I spent working in large
firms and now as a firm owner, I have climbed the
legal mountain one day at a time, avoiding sinkholes,
leaping over hurdles, and navigating around political
obstacles. I feel like a well-trained athlete on good
days and a broken down packhorse on bad days.
But, every day I am proud of my accomplishments.
So, why does the ad with the shirtless woman in the
white jacket and pants bug me? Maybe because I do
not want to associate bare breasts with legal work?
Maybe because this scholarly legal magazine had no
pictures of men without shirts or pants? Or, maybe I
am simply over-analyzing a simple picture? Maybe.

A couple of days after first seeing the

shirtless ad, I wrote an email to the Executive Director of the American Bankruptcy Institute (the magazine's publisher) and the president of the company depicted in the ad. I told them I was offended by the ad and why. I felt better after sending the email. The magazine publisher (a man) responded quickly, saying that many had responded to the ad and that it would not appear in the magazine again. The president of the company represented by the ad (a woman) did not respond. I could write an entire chapter about what I think of that woman's lack of response.

My lesson from this story: you need to speak up and tell people what you think (no shirtless women in legal magazines, please). Women are told again and again that they need to be likeable, but that should not foreclose us from disagreeing with the views of others and taking strong positions – to do so is to be a leader. It is risky to say what you really think if you are going against a perceived majority and there may be a cost to doing so. Several years ago, I participated in a meeting with the highest levels of global firm leadership where I worked (they were all white men who were older than me) and disagreed with all of them on the position the firm should take on a particular issue. After the meeting, I was told that I should not have disagreed because doing so would not be good for my career. A couple months later, the position I had taken ended up being proven correct – and on that day, suddenly everyone wanted me in meetings – my career was no longer in jeopardy. One person can make a difference; and, to rise up to the highest levels, we must not be afraid of confrontation.

Just ask Mary Barra, who became the CEO of General Motors in January 2014. After Barra's promotion, among other things, she was the face of GM during a couple of years when the company was criticized for its handling of faulty ignition switches, customer deaths, and auto recalls.[34] Barra reached the pinnacle of success in her industry and navigated through a year of litigation and Congressional hearings. Matt Lauer on The Today Show ignited a controversy during an interview with Barra when he asked: Can you be both a mom and a CEO and do both well?[35] Many said Lauer never would have asked a male CEO that question; I fall into that group. Lauer defended the question on his Facebook page, saying that he asked the question as a follow up to comments Barra made in a Forbes article and that he would have asked a man the same question.[36] In an interesting twist, Lauer's producer for the Barra interview, Tammy Fine, posted a response online on July 3, 2014, titled "Producer: Why I Wanted Matt Lauer to Ask GM CEO Mary Barra 'That' Question".[37]

Reactions to the Barra interview question and the shirtless woman ad are similar and reflect the subtleties we face today when we think about women in the highest levels of power. What is sexism and what is not? What questions can we ask? Are we treated the same as men? When does it matter? When should we be likeable and when should we say "no"? There are no easy answers. My best advice is: trust your instincts and speak truth to power. The conversation on all of these issues needs to continue so that the older women can remind the younger women how recently we attained their current power and so that younger women can remind older women that they still want to choose how to balance the power.

6

EMPOWERING EACH OTHER

What if every negative or hurtful word we utter acts like a boomerang that goes out into the universe, then turns around and hits us like a negative energy bullet? If this is the case, then a lot of folks criticizing Sheryl Sandberg might want to take cover. Regardless of what you think of the book Lean In,[38] in 2013 and beyond, its author, Sheryl Sandberg, got people talking about women's status in the workplace at levels not experienced since the 1970s. After hearing some women attack Sandberg on television, I read the book to determine what all of the fuss was about. I still do not understand what in the book triggered the negative remarks. Clearly this was a book written by a woman trying to help other women. So, why were some women attacking Sandberg?

Maybe, just maybe, some of us are resistant to anyone suggesting that we should act differently. We are so used to being independent and strong, that we do not react well when help is offered. Lean In offers help to women who are unaware of certain techniques or philosophies. Nonetheless, I can hear some women reacting to the points offered in Lean In: "I don't want to lean in" . . . "I already lean in" . . . "why is she telling me I have to lean in?"

Sadly, the harshest critics of women are other women. We begin by judging the outside of other women – "her hair is inappropriately long for her age" . . . "that color does not look good on her" . . . "why is she showing so much cleavage" . . . "she is not put together" . . . "she is trying to be too perfect". We also judge and condemn the way other women act – "she is too cold" . . . "she is overly friendly" . . . "she is a know it all" . . . "she thinks she is too good for us". Sound familiar?

Is there a scientific reason for our hostility toward other women? In her article "Why are women so critical of each other?", psychotherapist Rosjke Hasseldine writes that competition and jealousy among women are natural reactions when women are set up to survive in a culture where they are not equal to men.[39] She says that women survive on a starvation diet of invisibility and silence and are

43

in danger of acting like crabs in a bucket. As soon as one tries to escape and manages to get to the top of the bucket, the others pull the escapee back down because of fear of not being liked and fear of being alone. Dr. Seth Meyers says that in his practice, he sees female clients being critical of other women in areas where the criticizing woman appears to feel inadequate.[40] Dr. Sylvia Gearing says that women are naturally competitive, and will stab each other in the back routinely just to "stay even".[41] Wow! That all sounds pretty nasty, doesn't it?

Is there any way to put a positive spin on our behavior? I prefer to believe that women are complex creatures with such active, brilliant, creative minds that we are constantly searching for subjects to analyze. Like scientists and engineers, we consider everything around us, deconstructing the current status of a person or situation and comparing them to the way they could be if improvements were made. The definition of analyze is: to examine methodically and in detail the constitution or structure of something, typically for purposes of explanation and interpretation.[42] That is exactly what we do, right? Looking through this lens, women are not stabbing each other in the back, we are merely analyzing to facilitate improvement . . . sure we are.

We feel extremely comfortable analyzing others, but apparently, do not welcome analysis from others. If you want to ensure a swift hailstorm of criticism, give advice to women about the workplace. Why does this topic cause so much dissension? Perhaps it is because we resist being categorized simply by gender. Maybe if Lean In had been marketed as a guide for men and women on how to get ahead in a professional setting, critics would have been more kind. It is also possible that some women perceive the Lean In book as pressuring them to do something they do not want to do, or something they are not comfortable doing. To those women I say: don't' lean in. Lean back, if that works better for you.

Each individual woman is unique in her priorities, opinions and goals. Often, all women are lumped together and discussed as a gender, as if we are all the same. It is a mistake to assume that all women are the same and care about the same issues. For example, many believe that the number one priority for women in the workplace is the balance between working and spending time with children at home. Tell a woman without children or a woman with grown children that this is the highest priority for women and you may see her teeth grinding. The simple fact is that for some women issues related to children are important and for others they are not important at all.

I think Sandberg was trying to speak to a
group of women whom I have also met. There are
some women who want to achieve success in the
work place but wait for that success to be given to
them, rather than taking active steps to obtain it.
Lawyer women who want to achieve success must
be comfortable strategizing for it and asking for it.
Of course, there are exceptions. Sometimes lawyer
women are probably promoted easily without
specific planning, strategy and political wrangling –
but this has not been my experience, nor has it
happened to any of the women I know well.
Generally, things worth having do not come easily.
Most of the women I know first try to do good work
and accomplish the goals they think are necessary
for promotion (i.e., lawyers need to achieve billable
hour requirements and please others).   But
sometimes the expected result does not come, or it
doesn't come quickly enough, leaving us feeling
rejected. Marc Chernoff suggests using rejection as
motivation for change.[43]   Chernoff says that
"[r]ejection doesn't mean you aren't good enough; it
means the other person failed to notice what you
have to offer" and recommends using rejection as
motivation. So, if you are not achieving the success
you want at work, why not consider change? Switch
jobs. Start your own firm or business. Or, change

your behavior within your current work environment. There are no simple answers, but it is easier to control your behavior than to cause others to change their actions.

Do you feel like you are walking a tightrope while trying to juggle? The complexities of the workplace are obvious; less obvious are the spider web of difficult matters we manage outside of work. Some have spouses, parents or siblings with mental illness or dementia. For the women who have children in their lives, there are biological children, adopted children, and step children. In their spare time, some women are dealing with physically handicapped children, children with learning disabilities, or children who are gifted, but dyslexic. Again, all women are unique in how they handle and think about problem-solving.

But, one thing we have in common is that we can be really hard on ourselves. We think we should perform certain duties (like baking cupcakes for the party even if it means staying up all night to do it). We might think that we should be a particular weight (even if it means only sleeping three hours a night so that we can work out between 4 and 5 a.m.). Maybe we think that we are not successful if we have not been married nor had children by a particular age (who says we all have to marry or have children?).

SHERRI DAHL

Perhaps we wear pointy-toed shoes even though they hurt our feet and we hate them (if you like the shoes, you should wear them). Guilt, fear, pain, shame, anxiety, exhaustion . . . we should not experience any of these feelings every day. If you have little voices in your head suggesting that you are not good enough, tell them to be quiet, ignore them.

We all face a multitude of complex matters in our work and personal lives. Let's take care of ourselves so that we are prepared to be positive and mighty. Whether you choose to lean in or lean back, formulate your thoughts toward others and plan to achieve your personal goals from a place of positive strength. And never forget to reach a hand out so that you can help someone else. As you trudge into the future, follow the advice in the Katy Perry song and roar!

Rather than allowing ourselves to tear other women down, let's focus on empowering each other. Let's focus on our commonality and helping each other achieve goals that we never even imagined were possible.

7

OWN THE FIRM – TEN TIPS FOR GETTING WORK, KEEPING IT, AND GETTING PAID FOR IT

I blinked and 2016 flew by. My solo firm, Dahl Law LLC, was born in June 2015. At the close of 2015, I had been working for myself for six months providing legal services to large and small companies, individuals, pretty much anyone who would pay for an hour of my time. Heading into 2016, my first full year of working for myself, was exciting but there were many unknowns. Would I survive? Would I be able to pay my bills? As the primary financial supporter of my two twenty-something children and my mother, there was a wee bit of pressure. I once asked a principal in a woman-owned law firm in business for many years how long it took before she quit worrying about her firm's viability. Her answer was: "I will let you know when that happens."

What I did not know at the end of 2015 was that 2016 would be just fine. My business plan for 2016 was simple, including only two concepts: (a) keeping my overhead low by working out of my house and singlehandedly performing all the duties required by my firm from lawyer work, to IT and tech support responsibilities, to web design, and janitorial functions; and (b) marketing myself to referral sources and companies requiring varied legal help.

A big case was referred to me the first week in January. Then, another matter came in March, June, August, and November. As it turned out, the biggest issue in 2016 was not finding work, it was having enough time to do all the work that came my way.

Women ask me all the time: "How do you get the work?" Below are ten tips for getting legal work, keeping it, and getting paid for it.

First, the rate that I am able to charge working from my living room is much less expensive than any brick and mortar firm. Good friends in larger firms have referred several clients to me who cannot afford a bigger firm rate.

Second, there is no job too small (or too big) – I say yes most of the time. If someone wants me to review a contract for $100 per hour, I will do it. If someone wants me to prepare a will for $200-300, I will do it. I have spent most of my career helping large insolvent companies in bankruptcy handle issues including: (a) litigation; (b) tax problems; (c) contract issues; (d) employment matters – basically, any kind of problem you can imagine. I still help insolvent companies, but I also work for perfectly solvent companies – it's easier to get repeat corporate customers when they are solvent. For larger matters, I am building a network of attorneys who also work for themselves, who I can co-counsel with when a matter requires the attention of more than one attorney.

Third, there is no matter too far away. In 2016, I handled litigation in Missouri, Illinois, and all over Ohio. I negotiated more than 100 contracts with companies emailing and calling me from all over the world.

Fourth, weekends are not always time off. In 2016, I worked harder and more than at any other time in my career. For most of the year, I worked six and a half days each week. However, I must stress that working six days a week feels very different when you work for yourself. You wake up on that sixth day and say "Yay! I have so much work that I GET to work six days this week." Then, you do a little happy dance when you get paid for your work and get to keep ALL OF THE MONEY. Also, when you are your own boss, you can get a manicure or go Costco shopping during the week on your lunch hour. During the summer, I work on my deck.

Fifth, even when I am busy, I consistently market myself. When I am tired and all I want to do is take a nap, I still attend social functions, lunches and dinners. Also, when I talk to friends and colleagues on the phone or at social functions, I tell people about the work I am doing and what I am willing to do.

Sixth, I accept work, even when I want to take a break. There were times throughout the year, when I planned to relax and take a break "after this future court appearance" or "after I finish this next project". However, right before the case or project ended, new work would become available and I accepted it. There was one point during the year when I was so overwhelmed with work that I turned away a couple of matters, because there are only seven days in a week and you must sleep.

Seventh, I invoiced clients the way that I

would want to be billed. For example, when I have to perform extensive case law research, I reduce my hourly rate by 50% or so. And most travel time is not charged. Another question I get is "how do I collect money?" I accept credit cards and obtain retainers. As a business owner you must not be afraid to ask for money. No successful business person works for free. Often, I incentivize clients to pay sooner, by giving discounts for quick payments.

Eighth, I am accessible to my clients. My clients know that I work from home and that I answer my phone seven days a week 24 hours a day. OK, I have a couple of boundaries: (i) I do not answer work calls when I have had a glass of wine; (ii) I also do not answer calls when I am in the bathroom . . . anymore; and (iii) there have been a couple of really good meals I was just sitting down to where I did not answer a ringing phone. But, I am available at all times. Once, I answered a call on Sunday afternoon from a person who became a new client, that day, who had a mediation the next morning at 9:00 a.m.

Ninth, I do not work for clients that I do not like or trust, or who have an unethical agenda. Life is too short to work with problem clients. One potential client who called me in 2016 argued with me consistently during the first half hour that we spent on the phone together. After that half hour, I told him that I was not available to help him – my schedule would not allow me to work with him. I was busy, that was true. But more importantly, if a prospective client does not respect my opinion, or want to listen to my advice, during our first call, it is unlikely that the client will respect my opinion any more on the second or third call. Not working for clients whose values do not align with mine allows me more time to work with people who appreciate my help and who have reasonable and appropriate expectations.

Tenth, last but most important, I do good work. Whatever it takes to do good work, I do it. Sometimes doing good work means reading a hundred opinions looking for the needle in a haystack case. Usually it means extensive preparation. It means giving all of the cases the attention they require, even if several cases have deadlines on the same day. Looking at a problem or dispute from every angle. Learning about new industries and visiting the farm if you represent a farmer. Being patient. Fighting. Compromising. Not fighting the opponent at all, when that is what the client needs most.

Women achieve real power when they own the company. We are all capable of more than we can imagine. Women's Health USA 2012 reports that women make up 50.8 percent of the United States' population – we should be running at least half of everything! The National Association of Women Business Owners (NAWBO) provides that more than 9.4 million companies are owned by women. Women owned companies account for 31% of all privately held firms. Women of color are majority owners in 2.9 million companies in the U.S. One in five companies with revenue of $1 million or more is woman-owned. Approximately 4.2% of all women-owned firms have revenues of one million or more.

Have you heard of Sara Blakely? Ms. Blakely invented Spanx, a modern form of girdle or shaping and smoothing undergarment.[44] She considered becoming a lawyer but did not score well on the LSAT . . . twice. After a couple of months working for Disney, Blakely achieved success selling fax machines for Danka. Blakely researched and developed her idea for Spanx between 1998 and 2000 while she was a national trainer for Danka. Sara Blakely is now a billionaire. In 2012, Blakely was included in Time magazine's "Time 100" annual list of the 100 most influential people in the world.

Joanne (J.K.) Rowling, author of the Harry Potter series, was elevated from living on government benefits[45] to the best-selling living author in the United Kingdom and a Forbes reported first person to become a U.S. dollar billionaire by writing books (Rowling recently lost her Forbes billionaire status due, in part, to charitable giving).[46]

I am not suggesting that we should all aspire to being billionaires.

What I am saying is that we can do anything if we trust our instincts and gamble on ourselves. We deserve to be happy. Working at home is extremely inexpensive. Technology allows us to work from anywhere. Yes, I often work six days a week. But, I no longer eat as much fast food. Instead, I cook incredible meals, sometimes for breakfast, and almost always for lunch. I have better relationships with all of my family members because they see me more often. And I recently took a vacation – I hadn't been on vacation in six years. I am happy . . . every day. I am happy that I can help people, for an affordable price, and that I can pet my dog while I do it.

8

THE GLAMOUR OF OWNING THE COMPANY AND MARKETING IT

On a typical day, I am sitting at my desk, which is in the living room of my house, by 8am. This chapter addresses some of the questions regularly posed by folks about what it is like working from home. Yes, I shower every day before starting work, and no, I do not work in my pajamas. Early on, my clothes were more formal, even though I worked from home. It sounds silly now, but after years of wearing a suit to an office every day, it was unclear to me whether I would feel like a lawyer and act professionally on the phone if I dressed casually while sitting at my home desk. So, I ordered scarves and planned to wear business pants, a top, and a scarf every day. Online, I ordered 7 scarves of various color to wear throughout any given week.

Now, the scarves are piled neatly in my closet and I wear comfortable clothes while working, which means in the summer I wear shorts and in the winter I wear jeans or yoga pants. Guess what? While wearing shorts or yoga pants, I can still draft a complaint or motion and negotiate a contract or a settlement.

As it turns out, working for yourself is not that glamorous (who knew?). It is generally quite mundane and very similar to working for someone else. Throughout each day, I spend time analyzing:

(a) legal issues facing clients;

(b) accounting functions related to my law firm, Dahl Law LLC, which includes invoicing, collecting money, forecasting finances, paying taxes; and

(c) marketing Dahl Law LLC.

Advice provided to clients is enhanced, now, by my current perspective as a fellow business owner. Tax implications and other practical matters spring to mind much more quickly now. Clients, especially the owners of business, seem to respect that I, like them, own the company and therefore understand the broader implications of business obligations. Instead of simply providing legal advice, I feel more like a counselor or partner with the client.

I am typically at my desk until 8, 9, or 10pm at night, with breaks for lunch and dinner. Lest you think that there is no fun, there are days when I go out to lunch. One more thing – I walk my dogs three times each day. Yes, it is all very glamorous.

Other than my daily routine, the top three differences between working for a big law firm versus working for myself are:

(1) Control – I am in complete control of all things, now, including who I accept as a client, when I work on the matter, and how much I charge for the work. There are no arbitrary deadlines or unrealistic expectations from firm management. People considering working for themselves worry more than I ever did about this control issue. Often I hear "what if you do not know how to do something?" Really? You've never found yourself in a position where you do not know how to do something? You figure it out! You do research, seek input from others with experience in the area, and make a decision.

(2) Flexibility – In a large law firm, attorneys tend to get pigeon-holed into specific specialties. The firm encourages lawyers to specialize. For

example, I was a corporate bankruptcy attorney in a big law firm, and that is all I did. Now, the matters I handle are much more diverse. In addition to corporate insolvency matters, I form companies, sell companies, handle litigation matters, draft and negotiate contracts, and many other things. Learning new areas of the law is one of the joys of working for myself.

(3) <u>Lack of steady paycheck</u> – The security of a steady paycheck does not exist unless I create steady work for myself. That means that I am constantly evaluating my prospects for work. Do I have enough work right now? If not, what can I do to get more work? Who can I market to? What should I market? How should I market it? This is the element that frightens most people. They will not work for themselves because what if they cannot bring in enough work? I will let you in on a secret – even if you are at a large law firm, there will most likely come a time where your steady paycheck will end if you do not bring in enough of your own work. In the good old days (before 2008) a firm might have carried you through good years and bad for your entire career, but that is less likely now. Right before I started Dahl Law LLC, a law firm manager said to me "you have had two slow months . . . we would like you to separate from the firm". Right now, you might be thinking "that could never happen

to ME. Sherri must have done something else wrong." Yes, it can happen to you. And no, I didn't do anything wrong. It happens. If you work for someone else, you are rarely safe or secure.

During the ten minutes or so while I was being fired for the first time in my life (at age 45 after working and being promoted consistently for 31 years) I should have been anxious and upset – maybe even angry that this was happening without warning when I hadn't seen it coming. Instead, I was eerily calm. During the moments while I was being fired by this older white guy (let's call him Dick), the little voice in my head was saying "you will start your own firm . . . no more working for older white men . . . everything will be alright . . . this is for the best." As it turns out, Dick did me a huge favor. He backed me to the edge of the cliff and gave me the opportunity to fall back in faith – faith in myself, faith that although I cannot control all things, that I can handle everything that comes my way. Thank you Dick!

There are some who leave law school and immediately begin working for themselves. I salute them. They are fearless. In contrast, big law firms are wonderful places for teaching new lawyers certain skills. Things I learned from my big law experience include:

(1) <u>How big firms operate and how to compete with them</u> – Some of the clients that I service use me because they want big firm quality without paying the big firm price. Because I worked at a big firm, I market to companies by explaining the benefits of working with me versus a big firm. For example, at a large firm, my hourly rate in 2014 was $595 per hour, a couple of years later and working for myself, I charge $300 per hour. I charge less than the full hourly rate for legal research – big firms do not. I do not charge a full hourly rate for travel, like big firms. I accept credit cards for payment, most big firms do not.

(2) <u>Confidence</u> – I never feel nervous or worried about the skill level of any other attorney or business person with whom I may come into contact. In big law, I worked side by side with ivy league educated, extremely intelligent and successful people. We competed equally. In law, typically, all situations that might cause nervousness can be handled effectively with proper planning and preparation.

(3) <u>There are many ways to define "success"</u> – Some people think that working in a huge, international law firm means an attorney is successful. Would you still think that person was successful if they were miserable every day? If they

did not enjoy the work they did and did not respect their co-workers? If they felt as if the firm had been unfair to them by cutting their pay or not promoting them as others who were less productive were promoted? If they had so much work that they never were able to make time to participate in or enjoy family events? Success is not always obvious.

People always ask: How do you get work? There is no quick easy answer. The marketing net I cast for work is wide and it is never completely clear what is working best. My marketing strategies and tactics include:

(a) Website – I believe a lawyer and any business must have a website to appear credible and to allow prospective clients to research services (or goods) provided. I know that my clients review my website before they call me (they tell me so), even if they are referred to me by another lawyer. Less common, are the people who call me because they completed a random search on the Internet and found my website. The more common value of a website comes from a potential client first being referred to me by a colleague, then searching my name on the Internet, finding my website and determining that they are comfortable calling me because I have the skills they seek – or someone already knows me and needs my contact information. For example, a client living in a foreign country with a business in a state 3000 miles away, who worked with me at the big law firm, did a Google search to find my website and contact information after she learned that I was no longer at the big firm.

(b) <u>Written works marketed through social media</u> – Published written works provide instant credibility. Setting aside for the moment the fact that you learn a great deal by creating an original written work; in addition, written works provide a vehicle for communicating with people about your special expertise. For example, I published an article on municipal insolvency several years ago. To this day, I still receive calls from reporters in New York who include my views on municipal insolvency issues in their articles. Because of my municipal insolvency article, I was asked to speak at a national conference in Santa Fe, New Mexico, and have provided advice to insolvent municipalities. The value and usefulness of written works spans years into the future. There is a huge rush of interest immediately after the publishing of a written work, but far into the future, short quips with links to written works can be blasted out through LinkedIn, Twitter, Facebook and other social media. In short, a written work gives you an excuse to communicate with the vast sea of people on social media for extended periods of time.

(c) <u>Answering the phone and talking to people</u> – Some people say that half the job is just showing up. I agree. I talk to everyone and I meet clients everywhere. Last week, I was out of the country on vacation and ended up on a boat with 40 people that I did not know. While on that boat, I met a business owner from Ohio who, after talking to me, asked for my business card and emailed me the following week. Returning an email promptly and answering the phone when it rings is the easiest and sometimes the most effective form of marketing. Even if a call or email is not work related, prospective clients want to know that when they are in a jam, you will respond quickly.

Also, never underestimate the power of listening. A couple of years ago, I was on a trolley in San Francisco, and overheard a person talking on the phone – ok, in this particular situation, I was eavesdropping, but listening nonetheless -- after they hung up the phone, I handed the person my card and said "when that deal goes south, give me a call." I could tell that they were discussing shaky financial facts – information that they did not appear to understand was shaky. Six months later, they called.

(d) <u>Participating in groups and on boards</u> – Participating in social groups and on boards, particularly where the group plans an event, provides an opportunity for group members or board members to see how the other group members (like you) manage projects. There is an episode of the television show Friends where Phoebe is put in charge of bringing cups and ice to a party. Phoebe does all sorts of creative things with cups and ice. There was crushed ice, cubed ice, dry ice, and snow cones. There were cup hats, a cup banner, and other cup decorations. When I was a new lawyer, I volunteered to work on Bar Association committees and boards; this type of participation gave me early access to lawyers far beyond my experience level. Any duty I was assigned, no matter how mundane, I gave it my best effort, just like Phoebe. Bar Association colleagues got to know me and my work ethic and I learned a great deal from them. Having relationships with people, having them know that you are reliable, that you show up, that you do what is asked in a timely manner, and that you are creative -- is priceless. People are always judging. Allowing them to see you perform at a high level on a volunteer project puts you ahead of the pack in a competitive work environment in the future when they refer work or make hiring decisions.

The success of my solo practice is based on both traditional and modern forms of marketing. Corporate lawyers, traditionally, have not marketed with billboards, radio, print, or TV advertisements –

this type of advertising is more commonly used by personal injury attorneys. Traditional corporate legal marketing is based on relationships. Specifically, relationships built on trust; trust that you will win the case, trust that you will draft the correct type of contract, and trust that you will make the company look good. Today, I still must convey a credible image convincing potential clients that they can trust me. Modern forms of marketing, like social media, provides many opportunities for communication with a wide variety of potential clients. For example, I can reach out and touch potential clients who are known and unknown to me through Twitter, Facebook, LinkedIn, and blog posts on my website. Through social media, I can blast out articles on legal topics or my opinions on legal and business trends. There must be a balance of old fashioned credibility and relationship building and modern communication.

It is difficult to identify one form of marketing that is more successful than others; instead, all of the different forms of marketing work together. First, people need to know I exist, then, as a corporate lawyer, again, I need people to trust me. I am selling credibility. They need to feel comfortable putting me in charge of the lawsuit where they have been sued for $1 million or more; they need to believe that they are more likely than not going to be better off with me rather than someone else. It is unlikely that one form of marketing will convey all that a client needs to know before hiring me. Generally, the website is most effective after people have heard of me somewhere else. However, if they hear of me somewhere else, then want to find me, the website is the most effective tool leading them directly to my phone number or email address. Bottom line: the website, social media, and direct one on one human interaction all work together. Today, successful businesses need to use all of these instruments for marketing.

9

LET IT GO AND MOVE ON

Margaret Ann Bulkley (1789-1865) probably spent most of her adult life trying to avoid attention.[47] Born in Cork, Ireland in 1789, Bulkley attended medical school in Scotland beginning in 1809. At that time, women were not permitted to attend medical school or become doctors. Bulkley, aided by two benefactors, attended medical school using the pseudonym James Barry. She became a doctor, joined the British army, and lived the rest of her life as a man. Barry performed one of the first recorded cesarean sections in South Africa. After Barry's death, the person preparing the body learned that Barry was a woman. Barry's records were sealed until 1950. Bulkley/Barry did not allow the rules and policies of her era to keep her from having the job that she wanted.

College education is available to women today, in contrast with girls in the early 19th century. In 1833, Oberlin became the first coeducational college.[48] During the 20th century, graduate schools slowly began to admit women. In 1972, Congress passed Title IX of the Education Amendments, barring federally funded educational institutions from discriminating on the basis of sex and women's educational opportunities increased significantly.[49]

Carol Burnett lived through those days and with mysterious help became known to a generation of people watching television. Burnett was born in 1933 in San Antonio, Texas to alcoholic parents.[50] Her parents divorced in the late 1930s and Burnett lived with her grandmother, near her mother, in a poor area of Hollywood, California. The first of two mystery mentors helped Burnett after she graduated from Hollywood High School in 1951. Burnett received an envelope from an anonymous benefactor, containing $50, exactly the amount she needed for her first year's tuition at University of California Los Angeles (UCLA). She used the money to begin her studies. She planned to study journalism, but later switched to theater arts and English, with a goal of becoming a playwright. She had to take an acting class for her major. Invited by a professor to perform portions of a play with others at a party, Burnett performed and met a person important to her future. After seeing her performance, one of the party attendees, a man, asked Burnett about her future plans. She said that she would like to go to New York to look for theater work, but that she could not afford the trip. The man offered to loan both Burnett and her then boyfriend each $1000 interest-free. His conditions were that the loan had to be re-paid in 5 years, they must not reveal his name, and they must pay it forward by helping others pursue their artistic dreams. Burnett and her boyfriend both accepted the terms. After having success in New York theater and with many guest appearances on television shows, Burnett signed a ten-year contract with CBS. The contract required that for one year Burnett would be permitted to do any form of show she selected. The Carol Burnett Show was born in 1967, running until 1978. The network did not want Burnett to do a variety show, thinking that only men could be successful with the genre. The show received 23 Emmy Awards. Burnett re-paid the party attending benefactor and never revealed his identity.

In 142 years, we moved from a society where Bulkley/Barry had to pose as a man to attend college to a place where Carol Burnett was able to attend college in California despite her poverty. For both Bulkley and Burnett to succeed, they had to accept help from benefactors and make plans.

Admittedly, I am impatient because in my lifetime, I have not seen as much forward momentum in women's business and law successes as I would like. People do what they are comfortable

71

doing, I get it. You can't force someone out of their comfort zone if they do not want to move there. So many people I speak with seem unhappy in their jobs or in their marriages (you know who you are) and yet they stay in that place of unhappiness. There are many excuses: there isn't enough money, I don't want to be alone, at least here I know the environment, somewhere or someone else might be worse, it is a good job, they pay me well, people will think I am a bad person if I leave this job or this man, and on and on it goes.

To all of the unhappy women out there: You deserve to be happy every day. Yes, life is difficult, but you aren't supposed to be miserable, exhausted, or depressed every day. Nobody is perfect, and rarely is life easy, but it is interesting to hear some of the worries and stresses that tie people in knots.

A fundamental truth that people find hard to grasp is the following: sometimes you have to let go of something before you can find the better thing. An easy example comes in the form of dating. Do you know anyone who has been dating someone, for multiple years, who she doesn't really like? You ask her: why do you stay with him? She says: I don't like being alone. Answer: You probably won't find a better guy until you let go of the wrong guy; the wrong guy is taking up too much of your time. The same advice applies to many work situations. It is difficult to find the work you love if all of your time is spent doing work that you do not enjoy. If I hadn't made plans back in 1995, I could still be in the middle of the Mojave Desert working for minimum wage at a radio station.

Another truth that many unhappy people fail to accept is that you have to formulate a plan to get out of a bad situation (do I sound like a broken record, yet?). If your toilet stops working, you have to formulate a plan to get it fixed, right? First, you ask "can I fix it myself?" If no, then who can fix it for me? How much will it cost to fix the toilet? Can I afford to fix the toilet? Typically, the answer is you cannot afford not to fix the toilet, right? You need the toilet. So, you find someone to fix the toilet and pay for it even if you are short on money. Sometimes, a person will spend more time and money fixing a toilet then changing other parts of life that aren't working. Plumbers do not knock on your door uninvited saying "hey, is your toilet broken?" unless you call them first.

The same goes for jobs, boyfriends, and husbands. Ordinarily, a great job opportunity does not come to you unsolicited (ok, sometimes it happens; a great job came to me once, but that does not happen often). Usually, you have to exert effort to obtain a better job or a better partner in life. Both projects should be evaluated logically with plans formulated. First, let's discuss unhappiness at home, because work and home life unhappiness can be similar but it is sometimes easier to admit that your personal life is unhappy. Also, your life partner at home can create stress and tension preventing you from flourishing at work. I know. It is easy for me to say this – I don't really know your whole story. Yes, but I know my story.

The last year of my marriage was difficult. He was acting in ways that I did not like. I said things like "if you do that again, our marriage will be over!" Then, it happened again. I threatened again. It happened again. Doctors were telling me that he was mentally ill. Some suggested there were addiction issues. We received counseling from our minister. Before ending my marriage of nine years, I had to make peace with several core beliefs and issues: (a) a religious and moral belief that marriage is or should be forever; (b) the concept that marriage takes work and that you should not give up; (c) the notion that our children would be changed forever by divorce; (d) change – my life would change and I do not like change; (e) divorce represents failure; (f) things would be more difficult on my own with children; (g) loss of health benefits, because I would divorce the military; and (h) how would I support myself and the kids? Any one of those questions provided good reasons for not terminating the marriage.

Here is how I justified and allowed myself to end the marriage contract: (a) God would understand; God wants me to be happy; (b) I put real effort into the last year of my marriage; we had lots of counseling where I explained what I needed to stay – those basic elements were not provided by my husband; (c) regarding not giving up, maybe you have heard the cliché attributed to Albert Einstein that the definition of insanity is doing the same thing over and over again but expecting different results? (d) change can be good; (e) divorce is failure, move on; re-living a failure every day is worse than moving on from a failure; (f) yes, things are more difficult on your own with children; but in some ways it is easier to live without the burden of another person's issues; (g) losing health benefits is not the end of the world, you can get them another way; and (h) although there were some lean years while I was in college and right after law school, I supported the kids just fine by finishing college and becoming a lawyer after the divorce. At the time, ending the marriage seemed like the worst thing I would ever deal with in my entire life. It was bad, but as with so many giant life changes, you feel better right after you commit to change – it is like you pulled off the bandage quickly and accomplished something, a burden is lifted.

Similar advice is applicable when you are in a job that does not fulfill you. You should be happy, contented and fulfilled by your job. It is probably easier to stay in a job where you are not happy. Change is difficult. Apply all of the same items listed in the paragraph above to leaving a job or recovering from being terminated from a job. With the perspective of 48 years of living, with my fair share of highs and lows, I have found that when matters seem to be the worst, the lowest, and just plain awful, it is from those moments that some of the best changes occur – wonderful unregretted changes. Later in life, when things seemed bad, I started looking for the good that would follow and always found it.

Fear not. Don't be afraid of change. Don't be afraid that things will get worse. They might get worse, or they might get better, better than you ever imagined!

10
ASCENDING IN FAITH

Maslow's Pyramid is a psychological theory about the hierarchy of needs proposed by Abraham Maslow in his 1943 paper, A Theory of Human Motivation.[51] The five levels of Maslow's Pyramid reflect levels of needs in priority order from the bottom up: (a) at the bottom of the Pyramid, or the first level, are physiological needs of breathing, food, water, etc.; (b) the next level up on the Pyramid, level two, are safety needs, which are security of: body, employment, resources, morality, the family, etc.; (c) the third level up is love/belonging, which includes friendship, family, and sexual intimacy; (d) the fourth level up is esteem, which involves self-esteem, confidence, achievement, respect for others, and respect by others; and (e) the fifth and final level of the

Pyramid is self-actualization, involving morality, creativity, spontaneity, problem solving, lack of prejudice, and acceptance of facts.

Maslow theorized that when needs are not met, there is anxiety, and that a person must achieve all of the first four levels before self-actualization may occur. On the topic of self-actualization, Maslow concluded:

> Even if all those needs are satisfied, we may still often (if not always) expect that a new discontent and restlessness will soon develop, unless the individual is doing what he is fitted for. A musician must make music, an artist must paint, a poet must write, if he is to be ultimately happy. What a man *can* be, he *must* be. This need we may call self-actualization.

Maslow's Pyramid is an interesting way to order complex concepts about what motivates people. I don't necessarily agree that a person must meet the lower levels of the pyramid before reaching the higher levels. Achieving the lower levels are logical and rational, but not everything in life is logical or rational. Think of the artist, Vincent van

Gogh. He is considered one of the greatest painters, surely he was self-actualized, but he remained poor throughout his life, supported by his brother, unable to meet the first level of Maslow's Pyramid on his own.[52]

However, Maslow's Pyramid helps us to visualize that each of us has different incentive for our actions. As individuals we should grasp what motivates us. Employers or managers will benefit from understanding what motivates employees. If you ask five people why they enjoy working at a particular job – they all have the same job – you may receive five different answers. One may do the job because they like the salary. Another likes the schedule. Another enjoys freedom from direct management. Another is pleased by the title, or prestige, and on and on it goes. Some seek survival through a paycheck (level 1). Some enjoy helping others (level 5?)

Some women think that it is more difficult for women to achieve high levels of success in the world of business and law. It is easy for a woman to cite how women are disadvantaged, dis-respected, and kept from success. I do not want to minimize any theory for why women are disadvantaged. However, in some situations, level 4 of Maslow's Pyramid may suggest, in part, why some women do not rise in certain circumstances. Level four involves self-esteem and a feeling of achievement and respect from others. If a woman does not feel as if she has achieved what she thinks she should have achieved in her job, she will feel anxiety. For example, a woman at a large law firm, 12 or 13 years out of law school, who has not yet been promoted to partner, will likely feel significant anxiety. In her mind, she thinks "Why haven't I been promoted?" "Will I ever be promoted?" "The longer I stay the more embarrassing it is that I have not been promoted." "People will think there is something wrong with me." She may feel embarrassed about how her peers outside the firm judge her lack of promotion. Applying Maslow's theory, she will feel anxiety having not achieved the self-esteem level of the pyramid. Without the partner title, she feels dis-respected and is kept from reaching self-actualization. She may quit the firm, or move to another firm, to escape the anxiety.

How will a man react in the same situation? Some men will have the same reaction. Other men and women may consider the fact that they are making good money and just live with the lack of promotion. Some people may reduce the hours they work to punish the firm for the lack of promotion, in a passive aggressive fashion, but stay with the firm. Will a man feel the same sense of anxiety as the woman? If he feels that anxiety, will he leave? It depends. There is no simple answer.

Some women may feel more anxiety than men about not having been promoted, or not making as much money, because they attribute the slight to the fact that historically women are disadvantaged and they continue to be. In reality, the firm may be treating men and women equally as bad, but the men put up with it and the women leave. If you notice a law firm or company where women are constantly leaving the firm, it is possible that all people are treated unfairly at the firm, but the women are not putting up with it. It is also possible that women are treated worse. My point is that I believe many ambitious, the best and the brightest, women will not accept bad or unfair treatment for long.

If you feel anxiety based on unhappiness at work or in some other situation, consider making a change. Change is difficult. Change requires leaving the devil you know for the devil you do not know -- a leap of faith. The Merriam-Webster Dictionary defines faith as:[53]

(1)(a) allegiance to duty or a person: loyalty; (b)(i) fidelity to one's promises; (ii) sincerity of intentions (to act in good faith);

(2)(a)(i) belief and trust in and loyalty to

God; (ii) belief in the traditional doctrines of religion; (b)(i) firm belief in something for which there is no proof; (ii) complete trust; and

(3) something that is believed especially with strong conviction.

If you believe in God, as I do, then know that God wants you to be happy and that you will receive all of the help that you need if you are open to it and accepting of it. However, if you are sitting in a bad situation waiting for God or someone else to rescue you, then you better be open and listening very carefully to the help that is sent to you. There is an episode of the television show The West Wing where President Bartlet struggles with whether or not he should commute a death sentence.[54] The President does not commute the sentence even though he believes the death penalty is wrong. At the end of the show, the President is talking with his Priest. The Priest asks the President if he prayed about the issue? The President says that he prayed for wisdom, it never came, and he was upset about that. The Priest says that the President reminds him of the man by the river. The man by the river heard a radio report that the river was going to rush up and flood the town. And that all the residents should evacuate their homes. But the man said, "I'm religious. I pray. God loves me. God will save me." The waters rose up. A guy in a row boat came along and she shouted "Hey, hey you! You in there. The town is flooding. Let me take you to safety." But the man shouted back, "I'm religious. I pray. God loves me. God will save me." A helicopter was hovering overhead. And a guy with a megaphone shouted, "Hey you, you down there. The town is flooding. Let me drop this ladder and I'll take you to safety." But the man shouted back that he was religious, that he prayed, that God loved him and that God will take him to safety. The man drowned. And at the gates of the afterlife, the man yelled at God saying "I thought you loved me. Why did this happen?" God said, "I sent you a report, a helicopter, and a guy in a row boat. What the hell are you doing here?"

If you are working at a job that does not fulfill you and a recruiter calls you to ask if you are interested in making a move, what will you say?

If you do not believe in God, then focus on the non-religious parts of the faith definition and have faith in and loyalty to yourself. Be confident in your ability to handle difficult situations. Fret not. The time you spend worrying and feeling unhappy is wasted energy.

Humans have incredible survival instincts.

Amanda Berry, Gina DeJesus, and Michelle Knight were all held against their will, by Ariel Castro, in a Cleveland home for nearly a decade.[55] Each was kidnapped, raped repeatedly, and abused in other ways on a daily basis. Berry broke out of the house in May 2013, resulting in all of the women being freed. Castro hung himself in jail after being sentenced to life plus 1000 years – a coward's escape.

Ingrid Betancourt was a presidential candidate in Colombia in 2002, when she was kidnapped by FARC guerrillas and held captive for six years in jungle prison camps before being rescued.[56] Betancourt, Berry, DeJesus, and Knight all endured awful situations. They survived. On Maslow's Pyramid, for many years, each of these women were not having their first and second level needs met. Betancourt told Oprah Winfrey in an interview in 2010[57] that, in the jungle, she lost her fear – all fear. Apparently, she felt that she might die so often that she lost all fear of dying and thereby lost all fear . . . of anything.

On our darkest days, faith, religious or otherwise, can carry us through. If you are not a spiritual person, then you must have faith in yourself and your ability to handle the worst matters. You do your best, make plans, and move on. If you quit your job or get fired, you find another one. If you divorce your spouse, you move on. Have confidence in your ability to survive. Maintain hope.

If you believe in God or a higher being (or even if you don't) pay close attention to opportunities over which you have no control. Be open and receptive to unexplained gifts. Listen to the ideas that come uninvited from outside, deep within, or the voice that whispers to you. Be aware of the people who call to hire you or ask you to do something you were not planning to do. My life has been dramatically impacted repeatedly when I accepted opportunities that came unexpectedly. Usually, unexpected gifts come to me in the form of inspiration or feeling calm when it would be normal to feel anxiety.

At least once there was a gift given to me that I believe was a real miracle, similar to winning the lottery; but in my case, gifts are never more than I need, only exactly what is needed. Many, many years ago, before my divorce, probably around 1991, my then husband and I lived in California and our daughter was still drinking formula. We did not have very much money. We were poor enough that when we went to the grocery store, I had to add up the cost of food items, before we checked out, so that I could make sure I had enough cash to pay for everything. One night at the grocery store, I was in the baby formula aisle fretting because the soy formula that my daughter needed (she had allergies) was expensive. To get through until the next payday, I knew we needed one more can of the powdered formula, which cost $16, and we just did not have enough money. The little voice in my head told me to count the money in my purse again. So, I pulled out the cash in my wallet to count it again – although I knew how much money I had, because when you are that poor, you count your money often and know the location of every penny. But this time, when I counted the money, there was an extra $20 more than when I had counted the money at home before leaving for the grocery store. It was scary, because I had repeatedly counted my money before going to the store and I knew that I did not have the extra $20 an hour ago. Since that night in the grocery store aisle, I have always thought of that extra $20 in my wallet as a miracle; an extra $20 given to me by God when I needed it.

Many times inspiration comes from within and sometimes it comes from outside people who actually call me on the phone to suggest I try things that I ordinarily would not want to do. Twice, people have called me to suggest a job change. Although I wasn't looking for change, I listened and both opportunities resulted in significantly increasing my annual salary. On another occasion, a friend asked whether I wanted to go out one evening, I said "no". She said "Oh come on, go with us" and on that night I met my best friend and partner for life, Joel. For many years, the little voice in my head told me to write this book. I have argued with the voice, "I don't have time to write a book." Things happen when they should.

I hope that this book will inspire at least one person to make a positive change. Our individual actions impact other people dramatically. Without realizing it, our actions cause ripples in the lives of others spanning far beyond what we can imagine. My prayer for you is that you will take risks and try things that you have always wanted to do. That bucket list you have in the back of your mind – do it! Make plans, do good work, and help others. If you fail and have set backs (you will), or drop the ball, then pick it up again. Every day you receive another chance to do it all better and to ascend.

ABOUT THE AUTHOR

Sherri Dahl is the owner of Dahl Law LLC, a law firm representing primarily companies in insolvency, litigation, mergers and acquisitions, and general corporate matters. Prior to starting Dahl Law LLC, in Ohio, she was a Partner at Roetzel & Andress LPA, a firm of approximately 200 attorneys, a Principal at the law firm now known as Squire Patton Boggs, which at the time had approximately 1250 attorneys globally, and an Associate at McDonald Hopkins Co., LPA, a firm with approximately 100 attorneys at that time. Sherri also clerked for the Honorable William T. Bodoh, a bankruptcy judge in the Northern District of Ohio in Youngstown.

During law school, Sherri worked for Plymale & Associates, personal injury firm, externed for a Domestic Relations Judge, the Honorable Katherine Lias, clerked for the Ohio Attorney General Office's Chief Counsel and Public Affairs Sections, under Mark Weaver, and clerked for Nationwide Insurance Enterprise.

Before law school, in California, Sherri sold newspaper classified advertising, performed clerical functions for various companies, produced commercials and operated classic rock and talk radio stations, programmed telephone systems, supervised employees and purchased office supplies for a chain of retail window covering stores.

During and immediately after high school, Sherri was an Agriculture Lab Assistant for The Ohio State University, and cashier at Central Hardware and Wendy's.

Sherri has a B.S. degree in Business Management from the University of Redlands and a J.D. from The Ohio State University College of Law.

Dahl Law LLC was named to The Best Law Firms in America (2016) and Sherri was named to The Best Lawyers in America (2013-2016). Sherri was selected as an "Ohio Super Lawyer" by Ohio Super Lawyers Magazine (2012-2017); selected as one of the Top 25 Female Lawyers in Cleveland (2014-2017) and Top 50 Female Lawyers in Ohio (2014-2017). Currently, she lives in Northern Ohio with her life partner, S. Joel Chaney, her mother, Darlena, her two twenty-something children, Kodee and Jagger, and two schnauzers.

For more information, please visit www.sherridahl.com or www.dahllawllc.com

NOTES

[1] Calamity Jane Biography,
http://www.biography.com/people/calamity-jane-9234950#synopsis

[2] http://www.nawl.org/p/cm/ld/fid=506

[3] http://www.biography.com/people/madam-cj-walker-9522174

[4] Philip Galanes, <u>Ruth Bader Ginsburg and Gloria Steinem on the Unending Fight for Women's Rights</u>, N.Y. Times, Nov. 14, 2015, available at <u>www.nytimes.com</u>, https://www.nytimes.com/2015/11/15/fashion/ruth-bader-ginsburg-and-gloria-steinem-on-the-unending-fight-for-womens-rights.html?_r=0

[5] Naomi Sims, Encyclopedia.com, available at http://www.encyclopedia.com/education/news-wires-white-papers-and-books/sims-naomi-1949

[6] Available at https://www.facebook.com

[7] Information available at https://www.nwhm.org

[8] October 2011 Report of the Sixth Annual National Survey on Retention and Promotion of Women in Law Firms prepared by The National Association of Women Lawyers and The NAWL Foundation

[9] Female World Leaders Currently In Power, available at http://www.jjmccullough.com/charts_rest_female-leaders.php

[10] Virginia Commonwealth University, The Social Welfare History Project, Susan B. Anthony, available at

http://socialwelfare.library.vcu.edu/people/anthony-susan-b/

[11] Matthew McCoyd, From the President: In Memory of Judge Workman, DeKalb Bar Association News, available at http://dekalbbarnews.com/from-the-president-in-memory-of-judge-workman/comment-page-1/

[12] First Year and Total J.D. Enrollment by Gender 1947-2011, American Bar Association, available at https://www.americanbar.org/content/dam/aba/administrative/legal_education_and_admissions_to_the_bar/statistics/jd_enrollment_1yr_total_gender.authcheckdam.pdf

[13] Chris Boyette, 20 years Later: Key Moments From the O.J. Simpson Trial, CNN, available at http://www.cnn.com/2015/01/13/us/oj-simpson-trial/

[14] Ohio History Connection, Annette "Nettie" Cronise Lutes (1843-1923), available at http://www.ohiohistoryhost.org/ohiomemory/wp-content/uploads/2016/12/NettieCronise.pdf

[15] Oprah Winfrey, Thought for Today – Luck, available at http://www.oprah.com/spirit/thought-for-today-luck

[16] Out of Order At the Court: O'Connor On Being the First Female Justice, National Public Radio, available at http://www.npr.org/2013/03/05/172982275/out-of-order-at-the-court-oconnor-on-being-the-first-female-justice

[17] Biography of Sandra Day O'Connor (Retired), Associate Justice, available at

https://www.supremecourt.gov/about/biographies.aspx

[18] Sandra Day O'Connor, Oyez, IIT Chicago-Kent College of Law, available at https://www.oyez.org/justices/sandra_day_oconnor

[19] Maggie McLean, Arabella Mansfield: First Woman Lawyer in the United States, Civil War Women: Women of the Civil War and Reconstruction Eras 1849-1877, available at http://www.civilwarwomenblog.com/arabella-mansfield/

[20] Professor Cunnea, A Timeline of Women's Legal History in the United States and at Georgetown University, available at http://wlh.law.stanford.edu/wp-content/uploads/2011/01/cunnea-timeline2.pdf

[21] Myra Colby Bradwell, American National Biography Online, available at http://www.anb.org/articles/11/11-00095.html

[22] Joan Hoff, Law, Gender, and Injustice: A Legal History of U.S. Women, 164 (1991), available at https://books.google.com/books?id=45AUCgAAQBAJ&pg=PA164&lpg=PA164&dq=myra+bradwell+female+sense+of+innocence&source=bl&ots=ayRoNt42fl&sig=Yo1by_iHDp4VgjTHZHs_BQNpFpo&hl=en&sa=X&ved=0ahUKEwj78Kus_tbSAhVP42MKHbIfDv0Q6AEIGjAA#v=onepage&q=myra%20bradwell%20female%20sense%20of%20innocence&f=false

[23] Susan Stamberg, Female WWII Pilots: The Original Fly Girls, National Public Radio, March 9,

2010, available at
http://www.npr.org/2010/03/09/123773525/female-
wwii-pilots-the-original-fly-girls
[24] David Wallechnisky & Noel Brinkerhoff, 139
Female Soldiers Have Died in Iraq and Afghanistan,
AllGov, April 12, 2012, available at
http://www.allgov.com/news/us-and-the-world/139-
female-soldiers-have-died-in-iraq-and-
afghanistan?news=844316
[25] David Johnson & Bronson Stamp, See Women's
Progress In The U.S. Military, Time Labs, Sept. 8,
2015, available at http://labs.time.com/story/women-
in-military/
[26] P.J. Tobia, Defense Secretary Carter Opens All
Combat Jobs to Women, PBS Newshour, Dec. 3,
2015, available at
http://www.pbs.org/newshour/rundown/watch-live-
defense-secretary-carter-to-lift-ban-on-women-in-
combat-jobs/
[27] Available at
http://www.nytimes.com/2013/01/27/opinion/sunday
/kristof-shes-rarely-the-boss.html
[28] Ruth Bader Ginsburg, My Own Words 71 (2016),
available at
https://books.google.com/books?id=uiPyCwAAQBA
J&pg=PA71&lpg=PA71&dq=after+all,+land,+like+
woman,+was+meant+to+be+possessed&source=bl&
ots=S3BHTeDKgu&sig=1g40WM4RdQGsrq_ZY1
Xki8b6bvs&hl=en&sa=X&ved=0ahUKEwjeyo6xqd
fSAhXGyFQKHYwJC-
8Q6AEIGjAA#v=onepage&q=after%20all%2C%20l

and%2C%20like%20woman%2C%20was%20meant
%20to%20be%20possessed&f=false

[29] Lydia Lum, Breaking Barriers, One Person at a
Time, Minority Corporate Counsel Association
(MCCA) 2016 Survey of Fortune 500 Women &
Minority General Counsel, available at
http://www.diversityandthebardigital.com/datb/nove
mber_december_2016?pg=16#pg16

[30] Additional information is available at
https://www.2020wob.com/

[31] https://www.2020wob.com/companies/2020-
gender-diversity-index

[32] Commission on Women in the Profession, A
Current Glance at Women in the Law, American Bar
Association, available at
http://www.americanbar.org/content/dam/aba/market
ing/women/current_glance_statistics_january2017.au
thcheckdam.pdf

[33] Selena Rezvani, Large Law Firms are Failing
Women Lawyers, The Washington Post, February
18, 2014, available at
https://www.washingtonpost.com/news/on-
leadership/wp/2014/02/18/large-law-firms-are-
failing-women-lawyers/?utm_term=.903612a496a8

[34] David Muller, In Ignition Switch Debacle, GM's
Mary Barra Tells Employees: "We didn't do our
jobs", September 17, 2015, available at
http://www.mlive.com/auto/index.ssf/2015/09/in_ign
ition_switch_debacle_gms.html

[35] The June 2014 interview is available at
http://www.today.com/video/today/55512578

[36] Lauer's defense and the responsive comments are available at https://www.facebook.com/mattlauer/posts/780908178596828

[37] Available at http://www.today.com/parents/why-i-wanted-matt-lauer-ask-gm-ceo-mary-barra-1D79882023

[38] Sheryl Sandberg, Lean In: Women, Work and the Will to Lead (2013)

[39] Rosjke Hasseldine, Why are Women So Critical of Each Other?, June 14, 2008, available at https://www.sott.net/article/160153-Why-are-women-so-critical-of-each-other

[40] Seth Meyers, Psy.d. Women Who Hate Other Women: The Psychological Root of Snarky, Psychology Today, Sept. 24, 2013, available at http://www.psychologytoday.com/blog/insight-is-2020/201309/women-who-hate-other-women-the-psychological-root-snarky.

[41] Dr. Sylvia Gearing, Why Women Judge Other Women, June 4, 2009, available at http://gearingup.com/_blog/Gearing_Up_Blog/post/Why_Women_Judge_Other_Women/

[42] The definition of analyze is available at https://www.google.com/search?q=synonym+for+analyzing&sourceid=ie7&rls=com.microsoft:en-us:IE-SearchBox&ie=&oe=

[43] Marc Chernoff, Four Ways to Quiet the Negative Voice Inside You, undated, available at http://www.marcandangel.com/2013/07/25/4-ways-to-quiet-the-negative-voice-inside-you/

SHERRI DAHL

44 Clare O'Connor, Top Five Startup Tips From Spanx Billionaire Sara Blakely, Forbes, April 2, 2012, available at https://www.forbes.com/sites/clareoconnor/2012/04/02/top-five-startup-tips-from-spanx-billionaire-sara-blakely/#35f95e1b19b4

45 Christopher John Farley, J.K. Rowling On the Magic of Government Benefits, The Wallstreet Journal, Oct. 16, 2012, available at http://blogs.wsj.com/speakeasy/2012/10/16/j-k-rowling-on-how-government-benefits-helped-bring-the-world-her-magic/

46 Forbes Billionaire List: JK Rowling Drops From Billionaire to Millionaire Due to Charitable Giving, The Huffington Post, Dec. 13, 2016, available at http://www.huffingtonpost.com/2016/12/13/forbes-billionaire-list-rowling_n_1347176.html

47 Sarah Foster, Margaret Ann Bulkley (James Barry) (1789-1865), The Embryo Project Encyclopedia, February 11, 2017, available at https://embryo.asu.edu/pages/margaret-ann-bulkley-james-barry-17891865

48 Available at https://new.oberlin.edu/about/history.dot

49 Overview of Title IX of the Education Amendments of 1972, 20 U.S.C.A § 1681 Et. Seq., available at https://www.justice.gov/crt/overview-title-ix-education-amendments-1972-20-usc-1681-et-seq

96

[50] Biography, Carol Burnett, available at
http://www.biography.com/people/carol-burnett-9231937

[51] A.H. Maslow, A Theory of Human Motivation, Originally Published in Psychological Review, 50, 370-396 (1943), available at http://psychclassics.yorku.ca/Maslow/motivation.htm

[52] Vincent van Gogh, Biography, available at http://www.biography.com/people/vincent-van-gogh-9515695

[53] Merriam-Webster Dictionary, available at https://www.merriam-webster.com/dictionary/faith

[54] Available at http://www.westwingtranscripts.com/search.php?flag=getTranscript&id=14

[55] Crimesider Staff, Cleveland Kidnapping Victims Release a Memoir, Associated Press, published by CBS News, April 27, 2015, available at http://www.cbsnews.com/news/women-held-captive-in-cleveland-home-for-decade-release-a-memoir/

[56] How Ingrid Betancourt Let Go of Her Fear, Oprah Winfrey Interview, aired September 22, 2010, available at http://www.oprah.com/own-oprahshow/how-ingrid-betancourt-let-go-of-her-fear-video

[57] See id.

Made in the USA
Middletown, DE
05 April 2017